JOANNE RYDER

Each
Living
Thing

Illustrations by

ASHLEY WOLFF

GULLIVER BOOKS
HARCOURT, INC.
San Diego   New York   London

Library of Congress Cataloging-in-Publication Data
Ryder, Joanne.
Each living thing/Joanne Ryder; illustrations by Ashley Wolff.
p.   cm.
"Gulliver Books."
Summary: Celebrates the creatures of the earth, from spiders dangling in their webs to
owls hooting and hunting out of sight, and asks that we respect and care for them.
[1. Animals—Fiction.   2. Stories in rhyme.]   I. Wolff, Ashley, ill.   II. Title.
PZ8.3.R9595Wat   2000
[E]—dc21   98-51832
ISBN 0-15-201898-0

N M L K J I H G

Manufactured in China

The illustrations in this book were done in black gesso and gouache on Arches cover.
The display type and text type were was set in Goudy Sans Black.
Color separations by Bright Arts Ltd., China
Printed by South China Printing Company, Ltd., China
Production supervision by Stanley Redfern and Ginger Boyer
Designed by Ivan Holmes

To Jeanne McLain Harms and Lucille J. Lettow,
who care deeply about children and books,
teachers and authors, and every living thing
—J. R.

For Peri, who takes care of them
—A. W.

Watch out
for spiders
dangling in their webs,

for snakes who coil
and slither in the grass,

for toads who lurch
and leap across the road—
please stop to let them pass.

Look out
for wriggling worms
and creeping snails,
for darting bees
who dip among the flowers,

for streaming ants
    who streak the dusty trails—
    please step around
    their sandy towers.

Be careful
of snapping crabs
and swooping gulls,

of stinging jellyfish,
afloat and free,

of alligators
slyly drifting by,

and giant turtles,
circling in the sea.

Be wary
of bears
who linger in the dusk,

of owls hooting,
hunting in the night,

of bats who flitter,
whirling overhead,
and cougars pausing,
prowling out of sight.

Watch out
 for every living thing,
  for all beasts fine and free,
   who grace the earth
    and ride the skies
     and glide within the sea.

Be aware of them.

Take care of them.

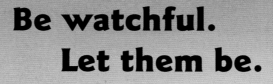

Be watchful.
Let them be.